writer's world

Published 2003 by Brolga Publishing Pty Ltd
PO Box 959, Ringwood Vic, 3134
markzocchi@brolgapublishing.com.au

National Library of Australia
Cataloguing-in-Publication entry

ISBN 1 92078516 7

Written by Di Berold
Photography and paintings by Bernadette Curtin
Design by Suzy Ditterich

Printed in China

Cover photograph *City Blue* by Bernadette Curtin

writer's world

Di Berold

To
Barney and Asher
and my parents, Ken and Robin

on writing

In Montreal, the snow came down in thick sheets that covered the city streets. Canadians call the first snow Winter Wonderland, but this was one of the worst blizzards in the city's history. I walked to the college I taught at through canyons of ice; the pavement had been cleared and salted so there was a narrow path on which to manouvre. Inside the old building, some brave students had arrived and scattered their books on their desks. Many were students with problems – histories of failure, addiction, psychological disorders – but each one was there because of a dream of a better future. We began talking about writing – not about essays or grades, but simply about the pleasure of creating. Everyone had something to offer – a diary, a few personal poems, the beginning of a novel. None of these was a set project. Each was part of the student's private world of writing.

The next year, in Australia – heat almost suffocated us in the classroom; the air was pungent with that characteristic scent of eucalyptus; cicadas seemed intent on battering us into a state of unconsciousness. I asked my students the same questions I had in Canada – 'Show me your writing. What else have you done? What are you working on right now?' Again, students spoke of diaries, joke books, favourite sayings, short stories and attempts at longer works. Lots of poetry was brought in the next day for me to read. I felt privileged to have access to their inner worlds, to their writers' worlds.

I have always written, too – letters, creative pieces, models for student writing, books on writing. I have my own writing sanctuaries – my parents' house in Queensland, a country place on the Mornington Peninsula and my town home with its light-filled study. I have always collected books and I love reading. What constantly amazes me is how many other people do, too – young and old. Beyond our daily life is a huge mosaic of reading and writing.

The other day my son sat down with his guitar and started singing a song he had composed – just for the sake of it. A handful of lyrics, another creative piece in its own right, evidence of ingenuity, a homage to the creative spirit.

This is the life-affirming journey we take in our writing and it's always there.

acknowledgments

I would like to thank Bernadette Curtin for her photographs and original paintings and Suzy Ditterich for the design. Their contribution has been invaluable.

To those who have always supported me – my family, colleagues, students and friends – I owe a debt of gratitude.

Divided into four sections *Writer's World*
contains useful strategies for writing from
the early developmental stages to a
completed piece.

Title ideas are suggested at the end of each
section and may be used as imaginative
triggers. Or you may wish to devise your
own titles. The book's philosophy is to
encourage your own creativity while
describing some of the technical aspects of
writing. The sections may be tracked
through in order or you can delve into
material that interests you. If you follow the
sequence set out you will have a developed
folio of original writing on completing
Writer's World.

how to use this book

contents

creating

expressing

communicating

prelude

How often have you said, 'I wish I could write'? Most of us write on a daily basis - lists, reminders, emails, letters - so it isn't hard to write. In fact, many writers use headings, lists and information to develop their stories.

There are many different kinds of writing - from short stories and poetry to longer fictional pieces and non-fiction.

Starting is easy. Encourage the feeling within yourself that you are creating, expressing, communicating.

Possessing an inner spirit of creativity is natural to all of us. Being in touch with that spirit is part of the joy of becoming a writer.

starter gear

Writing does not require expensive equipment. Many writers have only a small notebook or journal in which to record ideas, diary entries, bits of dialogue, jokes and sayings, observations.

a small notebook or journal
a variety of pens
a binder book
plastic pockets
folders
textas
coloured or design paper

Think of your journal as your eyes on the world – here you jot down pieces of reality, seen and heard. Assimilated into your psyche, such observed reality quickly becomes part of your own experience, your individuality.

Writers can write anywhere - in a room, in the garden, on a train, at a work place. Establishing a 'writing space' helps in developing a routine for writing. This may be a special corner in your house where you can enjoy privacy, an informal place for dreaming. An unusual lamp or comfortable chair or a cozy spot to play music helps to free yourself from your usual restraints – a mood enhancing space encourages commitment and creativity.

You may prefer to enter your ideas directly on to a computer in order to manipulate text and images, to experiment with ideas and layout.

writing space

I am a writer

'I can't write'. It's simply not true. Not many of us ever doubt our ability to talk or to interact meaningfully with others. Speech is fundamental to being human, something we begin as soon as we form our first baby words and improve as we grow older. And it is just a small step from talking to writing. It's most likely that the obstacle to writing lies in your mind not in your ability. It is within your reach.

think of yourself as a writer

you are also:

an observer
a reader
a collector
a correspondent
an initiator of ideas
a producer

inward journey, outward journey

writing interiors

But the vinyl chairs stick to your skin and a whirring electric fan makes it difficult to turn the pages of a book slowly. Windows and doors thrown open to catch a breeze also invite people. It becomes hard to live a quiet, solitary life.

The rooms in my mother's house, Olga Lorenzo

A good way to begin is to explore the realm of the known. Your deepest satisfaction and understanding come from those places that feel close and familiar to you. These are the interiors that reflect your own interior – emotions, experiences, hope. Once you describe places which are most intimate to you, the words will flow easily – the familiar will be transformed into the unfamiliar.

room to move

Rooms surround you. Mentally move from one to another. Make yourself comfortable. And begin. Describe this space. What feelings are provoked in you? What textures can you touch? What features are important to you? Do you sense the dark and the light, the old and the new? What encounters have you had here? What dreams have you dreamed?

■ **Jot down observations of:**

your bedroom

kitchen

living room

dining room

a sunny room

your study

bathroom

hallways

porch and verandah

probing the
meaning within objects

Within each room are objects and furniture possessing a
special meaning to you.

These may be:

a desk

a lamp

a chair

guitar

a football

jewellery box

collection of medals

stickers

a book

■ Describe your favourite pieces in detail, linking them to
their history and to their present place in the room.

objects

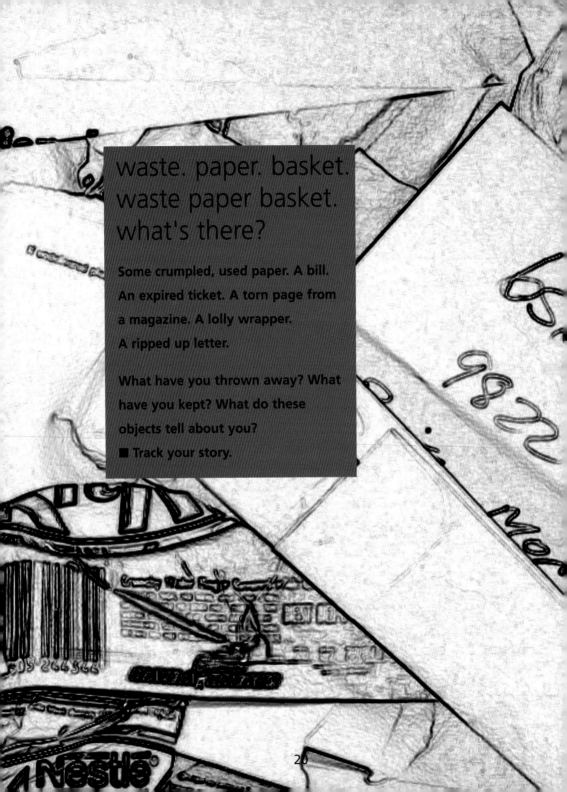

waste. paper. basket.
waste paper basket.
what's there?

Some crumpled, used paper. A bill.
An expired ticket. A torn page from
a magazine. A lolly wrapper.
A ripped up letter.

What have you thrown away? What
have you kept? What do these
objects tell about you?
■ Track your story.

collect, arrange, develop, produce

By now you will have collected some writing fragments which may be kept together in a folder or in your journal. These can become inserts for later stories, background material or short pieces in their own right.

★Title ideas:
Forgotten file
Knife drawer
Light on. Light off.
Bay window
Backpack

writing exteriors

The world outside presents endless opportunities for a writer and exists on several levels – boundaries, signs, paths and roads going elsewhere. When you describe the world outside, you have a unique view – just as your fingerprint, your voice and your appearance are unique, so too are your perceptions. No one else sees the world as you do or expresses thoughts in the same way. This is your strength, your secret weapon.

exploring the world

She walks up to the road and looks around. Everything is milky white and ghostly, like a stand of white-barked gums. Wattlebirds, magpies and honeyeaters fill the dawning day.

The rooms in my mother's house, Olga Lorenzo

descriptive sketches

backyard

fence
grass/ paving
clothesline
kennel
under the house

immediate boundaries contain
the space around the house

street

houses
curbs/footpaths
potholes
markings/signposts
names/numbers

walking down the street
introduces you to further
possibilities and extends your
range of observations

parks

swings/seesaws
trees
avenues
benches
conservatories

parks are intricate patterns
designed for enjoyment,
activity, contemplation or
simply so that you can cut
across the street

cityscapes

buildings	penetrating the boundaries,
squares/malls	the outskirts, you arrive in
nightclubs	the city which seems to
stations	emerge vertically from a flat
markets	plain
library	

riverviews

bridges	snaking through the city, the
banks	old river with its rough green
rowing sheds	edges makes its presence felt
boats	
jetties	

■ Descriptive sketches: Choose three or four sites to describe. Follow a real or mental map. You can unify these by placing a traveller in your scenes.

snaking through th
old river with its ro

landscape as a creative element

There's a half-moon tonight, etching the bleached stone of the city into the deep blue-black of its sky and shadows. People floated by like puffs of smoke.

Night letters, Robert Dessaix

of its sky and shadows

see dream
imagine in your mind's eye

land hills, rocks, plains

sea ocean, waves

sky still, wild, clouds, light

country farms, bush

The horizon grew a bloody rim through storm cloud. His watch had stopped. As the rain eased, the light hardened and he kept pulling on the oars, pulling, bracing himself with chants, with muttered shanties that robbed his breath

The multiple effects of rainshadow, Thea Astley

★**Title ideas:**

Inland to Uluru

Outback trek

Beach front

Shack on the cliff

Beyond the horizon

Koori legend

elements of writing

the power of words

You make me want to shout!

Johnny O'Keefe

Words are your ally. Be confident with words – read widely, know meanings. Scrutinise words for their sound and effectiveness. Vary the way in which you express yourself. Forget clichés – the sun set in the west, it was all a dream. Find your voice, your own way of saying things. The more you use and experiment with your writer's voice, the more confident you will become in your expression. Feel the power of the writer.

Words can be beautiful or ugly, serene or violent.

Investigate words:

**ALLITERATION
ASSONANCE
SOUND WORDS
EXPERIMENTAL WORDS**

Tip: Listen to music and write down some favourite phrases. These can appear as creative patterns in your stories. The same goes for poetry.

motifs
and repetition

> **Over and over he sings the words. Jirrbu-jirrbu.**
> **Lonely. Sad.**
> **Over and over and over, eyes fixed on the looming**
> **coast, he sings all the way to the mainland.**
>
> *The multiple effects of rainshadow,* Thea Astley

Repeating a word, phrase or sentence gives rhythm to writing. Like the beat in music, rhythm is hypnotic. Not knowing quite what to expect engages us.

Word: Mind-numbing. Mind-crunching.

Phrase: All a trick. All broken promises. All in a heap.

Sentence: I wanted to go. I wanted to stay. I wanted to jump.

**Repetitions
can occur next
to each other
or can indicate
new sections
of the story**

The door formed a narrow V
The door stood open
The door was tightly shut

■ Write a story beginning or ending each paragraph with a repeated sentence or variation on a sentence. Concentrate on rhythm.

★Title ideas:
broken promise
the door
mind games
a day of thunder
falling star

imagery

At its simplest, an image is something you can see or sense. Imagery defines your view in an individual and powerful way. Images may be of sight, sound, smell, touch, taste. Images are among the strongest tools you can use as a writer.

■ Take a journey to a national park. In the wilderness, write impressions of everything you see and hear. Crush a leaf and smell it. Feel the bark of a tree and describe its texture.

In the wet sand by her foot, a bit of colour catches her eye. The glass is green, pale and cloudy, the colour of lime juice that has been squeezed into a glass. She brushes the sand off and presses the sea glass into her palm, keeping it for luck.

Sea Glass, Anita Shreve

■ Do the same in a city cafe or at the docks. Observe the café crowd, the smell of food and coffee. Or write a description of the wharves and the sea as if you were painting it in words. Inhale the salt air or note the smell of oil. Feel the old wood of the pylons.
This kind of actual writing gives your descriptions authenticity and focus.

see hear sme

symbols

Symbols are a kind of shorthand. There are many symbols we routinely recognise and using these gives added resonance to your writing.

cross	Christianity, suffering
red rose	love/ passion
white lily	death/ purity
garden	Eden

discover the word 'archetype'

Symbols are often used to reflect a state of mind. For instance, a glass symbolises a state of fragility - the shattering of the glass vividly illustrates a moment of extreme crisis or madness. If you replace 'She went mad' with 'The glass fell to the floor and shattered', the original idea becomes more subtle and intense!

■ Choose an object with a symbolic value and trace this object through your story.

touch taste

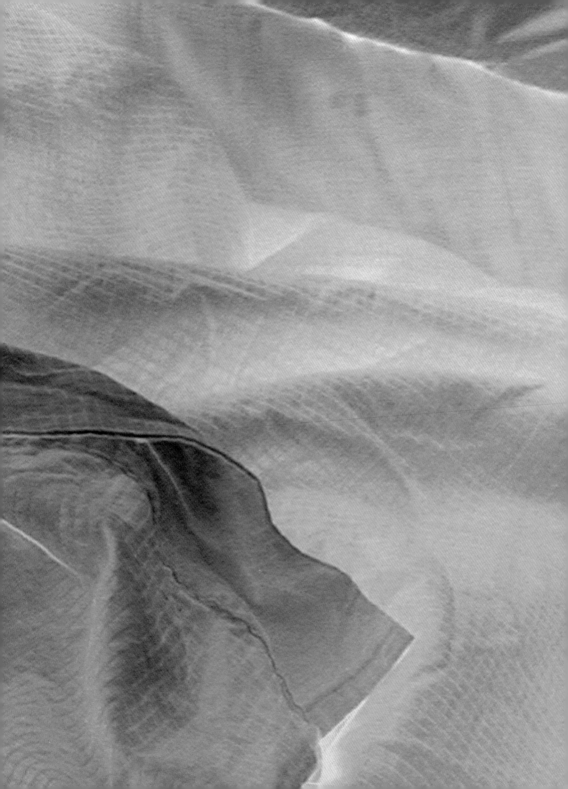

the silk wrap

A mother wears an old silk wrap from a second-hand shop.
There is a crisis in her life (a drug addiction, a theft).
When the crisis erupts, she pulls the silk wrap tightly around
her, but she feels no comfort.

Metaphor: a sea of anticipation
love is a volcano

Simile: the crane is like an insect
wordless and weightless as a sigh

■ Draw up your own list of favourite metaphors and similes.

★**Title ideas:**
  The silk wrap
  Shattered glass
  'Roses are red, violets are blue'
  The tattoo
  Garden of dreams
  The ring

portraits
developing character

real lives
imagined lives

**Real lives/ imagined lives - The lines
between reality and imagination are blurred.**

At the heart of a story are the characters who animate your
imagined world. Stories are driven by the characters you create
and we are drawn into their lives.

- **Choose characters drawn from
  real life - portraits of your
  family, friends, relatives, neighbours**

- **Explore imagined lives - a couple in the
  park, a builder on a construction site, a
  traveller on the train, two people in a
  crowd, musicians in a band, a child.**

your approach to character
draw a concept map

Feel the character slowly taking shape in your mind. In your journal, bring them to life.

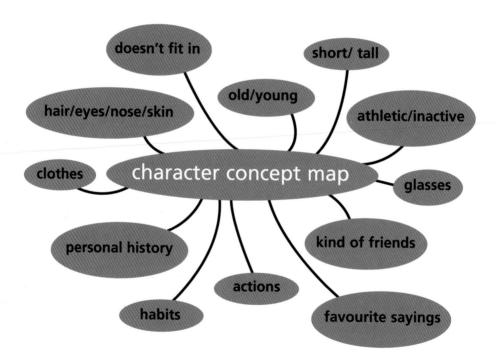

doesn't fit in

short/ tall

old/young

hair/eyes/nose/skin

athletic/inactive

clothes

character concept map

glasses

personal history

kind of friends

actions

habits

favourite sayings

■ **Describe one or two characters:**
  - **track their movements**
  - **what motivates them? How do they change?**

■ **Follow a character through a day:**
  - **character in initial stages**
  - **development or complication**
  - **character in final stages**

★**Title ideas:**
  The friend
  Neighbours
  Photo album
  Memories
  A working day
  Travellers

establishing mood
and emotional depth

Blow, winds and crack your cheeks! rage! blow!

King Lear, William Shakespeare

Changing mood and tone gives excitement and intrigue to your writing and keeps your reader guessing. Probe the mood or emotional state of your character. A change of emotion provides a roller-coaster effect. Hey, where are we going?

■ **What would be different in your story if you introduced the following elements?**

love   hate

joy   grief

acceptance   fear

hope   regret

■ **Write a short piece demonstrating contrasting feelings –
a character moves from fear to acceptance.**

gymnast   hospital patient   athlete   explorer cook builder lover soldier

a writer's trick

■ **Link the emotional mood to an external element - weather, time of day, kinds of light. This is a great way to intensify the ambience of your writing.**

■ Develop a block of description on:

storms and wild wind	noon
fog and mists	midnight
changing winds	dawn
blazing sun	afternoon
clear skies	morning

■ This is how you do it. When shaping a story, track through different moods in your character and change the external environment to match.

angry person	happy person	fearful person
wind gathering	sun shining	storm breaking

Any landscape elements - dark, threatening rocks and wheat-coloured plains – may be used to express emotional states.

Use other writers as models – read their work to see how they do it

contrast and conflict

Two households, both alike in dignity
In fair Verona, where we lay our scene
From forth the fatal loins of these two foes
A pair of star-cross'd lovers take their life.

Romeo and Juliet, William Shakespeare

Two households, bot
In fair Verona, where
From forth the fatal
A pair of star-crosse

contrast

Yin and yang. Opposites create strength and tension in your writing. So, add a zest of lemon to your fizzy drink!

Zigzagging patterns:

happy	sad
peaceful	dangerous
joking	serious
light	dark

■ With a texta, colour the emotional shifts in your story.

conflict

■ Characters need to crackle. Decide what connects them and what divides them. When does the initial moment of conflict occur? What causes the crisis?

clouds collide causing thunder

Conflict is based on:
A physical or mental struggle
Different attitudes
Separate goals or both wanting
the same goal to the exclusion of
the other
Different races, cultures, religion–
a multicultural environment

■ **In your journal:**
Describe two characters
♦
Establish a point of conflict
♦
Describe their reconciliation
or
Failure to reconcile

★**Title ideas:**
Meeting in Jerusalem
New York subway
Behind the fence in a
refugee camp
'He wasn't good enough for
my family'

irony

levels of writing - beneath the surface

'I knew him best.'

'You knew him best,' I repeated. And perhaps she did. But with every word spoken the room was growing darker...

Heart of Darkness, Joseph Conrad

Irony: the actual meaning is the opposite of the intended meaning.

surface
• • •
underneath

■ Using irony, develop a piece exploring two characters and their actions.

■ Write a story with an ironic - or unexpected - twist at the end.

Dramatic irony: In a play, the audience knows what is going on but the characters do not.

ironic

satire

the use of sarcasm and ridicule to expose human folly

When my mother explained to him that I had gone over the top of the playground swings making a 360-degree loop and had been knocked unconscious twice, Dr Laughton dutifully wrote down all this information, laid down his clipboard with certainty, and said that I had worms and needed Fletcher's Castoria.

Too close to the falls, Catherine Gildiner

irony
ridicule
wit
expose
denounce
deride
criticise
vice
folly
absurdity

satyr: a mythical
Greek creature
that is part
man/ part goat

★ Title ideas:
Just my luck
Fun and games
Profile of a leader
The fable
Close call
Reality check

dialogue

Happy talk, keep talking happy talk...
South Pacific

Authentic dialogue brings
your characters to life in
unexpected ways. The
impact of a shared
conversation is immediate
and compelling

Types of dialogue:

formal an exchange between politicians or officials
informal a chat between friends, a family conversation

conversation starters

■ Begin with small scraps of 'talk' – try role-playing your
dialogue with a friend to ease out any stiffness.

formal
An employer has a discussion with an employee who is about to be fired.
An applicant is interviewed for a job by a consultant.
A Member of Parliament presents a submission on developing a new park
or a proposed freeway to a committee and fields questions.
A Customs Officer questions a traveller at the airport.

informal
A girl and a boy have just met.
A father discusses his problems with his family at breakfast.
A brother and sister argue.
Two friends stand on a bridge and talk about their lives.

■ Have a go - Explore accents or
idioms using a sequence   of
dialogue. Experiment with the
way people talk. Lots of
writers copy scraps of overheard
conversations in their journals to
use later in their stories. You
can, too! Try an extended
dialogue that could become a
play or film.

who is speaking?

Imagine you are in the mind of your character. An important choice needs to be made before you start - who is 'speaking' in the story?

This can be:
I: first person
you: second person
he/ she: third person
or
someone outside events who sees
everything, also known as the
omniscient narrator.

actor pilot witness me

★ **Title ideas:**

'**Acting was all I dreamed of.**'

'**Your plane looked silver against the sky.**'

'**He was the only witness.**'

who is listening?

Your next experiment is to adjust your writing style to suit your listeners, your audience. They want to share your world.

■ **Have a go: a children's story for a young audience**
a series of letters to someone your age
a story for an adult audience
an autobiography for publication

experiment. point. view.

writing sketches

■ Using 'I', write a paragraph describing an event - a burglary,
an accident -
'I saw the black hands on the window pane' - 'I heard the sickening thud of the impact'.

■ Choosing the same idea, use 'you' –
'You gasped when you saw him'.

■ Then try he or she –
'He was dead sure he heard a sound'/ 'She felt fear rise in her'.

■ Finally, the 'all-seeing' method –
'The house looked threatening in the darkness. Those inside slept peacefully'.

It's easy to see how dramatically the impact of your writing can change as you alter who is speaking or the viewpoint. So, experiment with different viewpoints in the same piece - this can be a bit of a brain-stretcher! In contemporary writing, swapping viewpoints is called the multiple narrative.

51

interior monologue

The thoughts inside the observer's head are called interior monologue - self-talk or observation that no-one except the reader can hear. You are in control of these thoughts.

Model –
I wondered about my capacity for this job. When it came down to it, I sometimes found myself floundering, like a fish out of water. My friends think of me as a pretty cool customer, I know that, but they didn't grow up with my father, a man who could destroy your ego in ten seconds flat.

■ Taking your time, write an interior monologue to express the thoughts of your character (who could be you in disguise).

context

Characters do not exist in a vacuum. Describing social or historical context anchors your characters in time and place.

When Sonny Tay was conceived in 1968, momentous events had been taking place around the world: the Prague Spring, the Paris May Days when the trade union workers struck and students proclaimed that it was forbidden to forbid, civil rights marches and the death of Martin Luther King...

Love and Vertigo, Hsu-ming Teo

■ Check out some sources to help you research context, then write a description of the era you have chosen. This may seem time-consuming, but it's worth the effort!

exploring viewpoint
click!

Imagine that you are a photographer taking a photograph of a scene. This is the scenario.

> A man and a woman sit at a table outside a restaurant drinking coffee. You compose the scene – look at the derelict rubbish bins, see how pigeons arrive to pick up crumbs of food. You observe how a breeze slightly lifts the hem of the woman's skirt. Now the man leans forward to speak softly in her ear. Click. The moment is frozen. The photograph describes the caught moment.

In the same way, a writer describes a still point in time and then steps back to comment on what has been seen.

★Title ideas:

Café scene

Postcards

Inside the gallery

Courtroom encounter

describe scene

the observer describe thoughts

Story arc

A. Describe the scene. The time is noon.

B. What does the observer see?

C. What are the thoughts inside the observer's head?

D. The scene moves on in time. It is now one o'clock.

■ A series of photographs or magazine
cuttings may also be used for this exercise.
Place three postcards on a bench in a sequence
and describe them without filling in the gaps.
Create a title.

dimensions

the writer is a camera

A camera has the ability to move in different ways - so does the writer. Think of a photo of a person or landscape in long distance, then a middle distance shot and finally a close-up. Your writing can do the same thing.

■ Describe a landscape - mountains rolling down to the sea.
  Describe two people walking along the path parallel to a cliff.
  Describe each of the characters in detail.
  Return to the original landscape.

Positioning the eye of the writing:

A camera can take a shot from above, below or within. A good writer copies these techniques.

close-up

He moved always on these two levels, through these two worlds: the flat world of individual grassblades, seen so close up that they blurred, where the ground-feeders darted about striking at worms, and the long view in which all this part of the country was laid out like a relief map of the Shire Office – surf, beach, swampland, wet paddocks, dry, forested hill-slopes, jagged blue peaks.

Fly Away Peter, David Malouf

bird's eye view
view below
view within

view

Bird's eye view

Describe a building or a paddock as if
you were flying over the top of it.

The view below

Write a piece from street level, looking
up at roof-lines.

The view within

Imagine you are lying in a field of grass
and describe what you see - stalks,
insects, seeds.

■ Your turn

Choose a view that is special to you and describe it from
three different viewpoints.

★ Title ideas:

Homestead. Paddocks

The sound studio

Ski slopes

Surf odyssey

the element of time

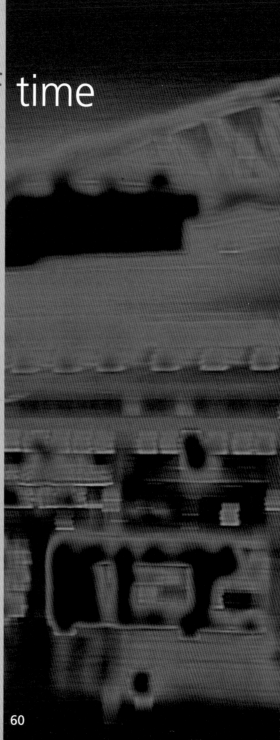

Time has several dimensions - past, present and future. You are in charge of the time machine.

past

She played in the sand-pit with her brother

present

He notices how quickly he is riding his bike

future

They will wonder what it will be like to be old

Memory and flashback deepen time.

Stream of consciousness – thoughts rolling out without punctuation is another trick writers use.

Check out James Joyce or William Faulkner.

historical fiction

There is a richness in the past, in the details available to us through history. All of history is open to you as a backdrop for your stories – from the moment that has just passed. For extra authenticity, read books on history, check old maps of cities, review art, culture, class systems, social history, war. You are a collector of ideas, an inventer.

contemporary writing

You belong to the present. You have a unique insight into what being alive now means, so grasp this moment of time. Use the energy of the present to infuse your observations – your place, your world, your thoughts, your time. Go anywhere in your world, experiment with the voice you know.

science fantasy

What is more intriguing than wondering about the future? What is outer space like? Will we colonise Mars? Do parallel worlds exist? The possibilities are endless. Writers and filmmakers use science fantasy to project our dreams and anxieties, even our nightmares. Feel the awe of the future, the mystery of fantasy. Indulge your imagination.

■ Parallel worlds: Write a story that moves backward and forward in time and space.

Hawkheel remembers his past

Hawkheel's face was as finely wrinkled as grass-dried linen, his thin back bent like a branch weighted with snow. He still spent most of his time in the fields and on the streams, sweeter days than when he was that half-wild boy who ran panting up the muddy logging road ...

Heart songs, E. Annie Proulx

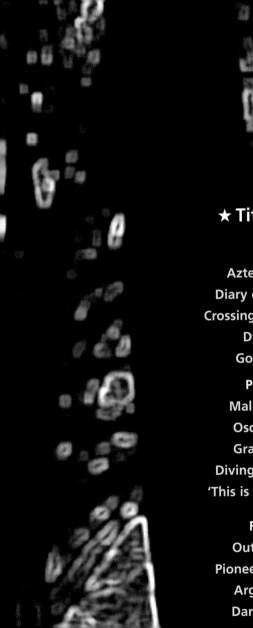
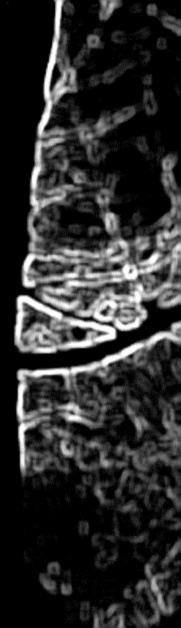

★ Title ideas

Past
Aztec Temple
Diary of a Queen
Crossing the Atlantic
Dynasty
Gold fever

Present
Mall cruising
Oscar night
Grand Final
Diving in Broome
'This is where I am.'

Future
Outer space
Pioneers on Pluto
Argon alert
Dark station

bay disaster

Story 1 (present)

The man is silent
The man goes to work
The man sees boats on the bay
The man goes home to his family

Story 2 (past)

The man as a boy is talkative
The boy helplessly watches a
friend drown
The boy refuses to speak

Interweave the stories, placing the past story in italics.

The father is silent - Story 1

The boy is talkative - Story 2 (italics)

The father goes to work - Story 1

The boy helplessly watches a friend drown - Story 2 (italics)

The father sees boats in the bay - Story 1

The boy refuses to speak - Story 2 (italics)

The man goes home to his family - Story 1 – finally, he is
able to speak to his daughter.

■ Cross-cut two parallel stories in this way, building up
character and landscape details as you go. It's an exciting
method to try!

interweave

beginnings

Writers want to create an initial impact in their stories, that first shiver of recognition, like an iceblock slithering down your spine. A successful start reinforces the delight of knowing you are in for a reading treat!

And there is nothing more satisfying than a good ending – an ending rounds the story off, provides a contrast to the beginning or leaves the future in the air (the ambivalent ending, where you fill in your own reading of the story).

■ When in doubt, end on a decisive action –
He walked away. I heard the sound of his shoes on the footpath.

■ Or incorporate an imaginary question mark –
Nothing would ever be the same again. The world had shifted slightly.

endings

beginnings

When I was twelve years old God spoke to my father for the first time. God didn't say much. He told my father to be a painter, and left it at that, returning to a seat amongst the angels and watching through the clouds over the grey city to see what would happen next.

Four letters of love, Niall Williams

As I begin to tell this, it is the golden month of September in southwestern Ontario. In the splendid autumn sunshine the bounty of the land is almost overwhelming, as if it is the manifestation of a poem by Keats.

No Great Mischief, Alistair MacLeod

These are the myths I tell about my family and, like all myths, they are both truths and lies –

Love and Vertigo, Hsu-ming Teo

endings

Till here, as on other beaches, in coves all round the continent, round the vast outline of it, the heat struck of a new day coming, the light that fills the world.

Dream stuff, David Malouf

He wore scuffed cowboy boots, faded jeans, and a torn black shirt with a cactus embroidered on the back, and the heel of his hand beat out a Tex-Mex rhythm on the cracked steering wheel.

Heart songs, E. Annie Proulx

■ Have a go: Write a series of beginnings and endings, taking no more than five minutes each.

the fragmented story

SCENARIOS

A technique to give a story interest is to write it in pieces, to keep your reader in suspense. There are several easy ways to do this.

Scenario A: A house is up for sale. Several characters see the same house in different ways.
1. The house is described by the grandmother who lived there forty years ago.
2. The house is described by the auctioneer at the auction.
3. A hopeful young couple having problems in their busy lives describe what they expect from the house they have bought.

Scenario B: An accident occurs. The accident is seen from different perspectives.
1. A feature article is written by a reporter on increasing driving fatalities at Gunner's Corner.
2. A policeman writes a report on an accident at Gunner's Corner.
3. A girl is driving, dreaming about her new life. She approaches Gunner's Corner.

■ Respond to Scenario A or B
   or
■ Construct your own scenario by choosing an intriguing object, place or event.
   Describe it from two or three different viewpoints.

HEADINGS AND SUB–HEADINGS

Headings can be striking and provocative – good headings indicate changes in time and place. It's a kind of shorthand to keep your writing sharp and focused.

Los Angeles, 8 am

New York, midnight

- Write your version of possible events, located in two cities of your choice.
- Devise your own headings and write up the story to fit.
- Or chop up one of your existing pieces.

Tip: Don't worry about filling in all the bits between. Simply 'be there'.

FRAMEWORKS

Giving your story a frame adds to the feeling that your piece is structured and well-plotted. And it's fun! Start with a description of an event or character in the present, write most of your story in the past and return to the present. You may want to use alternating locations.

Format	Example
Introductory frame (in italics)	On a train travelling to Sydney - getting on train at Melbourne station
Main story (plain font)	Flashbacks to events in past in a different setting
Intertwine with events on train – sound of whistle, roar through tunnel	
Concluding frame (in italics)	On a train travelling to Sydney - approaching destination

Using italics gives emphasis to the structure of your story.

[START FRAME]

MAIN STORY (no italics)

[RETURN FRAME]

The experimental option – flaunt the rules! The design is yours to create.

★ Title ideas:

Interstate train

Safari

Rebellion

Dreamtime

Betrayal

bringing it
together

You now have your technique for writing landscape, character, dialogue and interior monologue in place. Think of a good story with a point of conflict between two characters. Who are they? Where are they? What is the weather like? You don't need to have everything worked out at this stage, just an idea of where you're going. Here is a model which will work for a short story which you can adapt. At first, spend just a short time on each section and keep it fairly simple. Polishing it up comes later.

format

Landscape	Lake and hills/ weather
Character 1	Describe character 1 (real or imagined)
Character 2	Describe character 2
Conflict	Character 1 meets character 2
Discovery	Use dialogue/ emotions/ actions
Interior monologue	Thoughts of character 1
Decision	Character 1 acts
Final action	Character 2 departs
Landscape	Return to beginning - but change has occurred - time/ weather

■ You will have about ten paragraphs of rough copy. Go through it, change details, work on the impact of your story and its final design. Give your story a title.

★Title ideas:

The meeting

Ripples on the lake

The Great Divide

Feud

Seasons

Vanishing point

the meeting

you are a story teller

The classic storytelling technique is one where landscape and characters are introduced followed by a rise and fall in the action. In movies, a car chase signals a film convention. After the excitement of the chase, the action falls again – this can be a rescue or the resolution of a love affair.

character & setting
conflict
chase/climax
rescue
ending: resolution of conflict

■ Write a short outline, following this format. When you are ready, expand
your outline and refine the details of your story. To provide depth and
interest, add some interior monologue for your central character. Give the
final piece a zappy title.

★**Title ideas**
   The assignment
   Day of reckoning
   Near miss
   Promise me this

story

genre

■ Discover different types or genres

poetry

wordscape

haiku

sonnets

performance poems

songwriting & lyrics

scripts for films & plays

short stories

nonfiction & reports

autobiography/biography

interviews

feature articles

editorials

e-mails

novels

historical
Gothic/ horror
murder/ mystery
adult/ adolescent/
children
contemporary
science fantasy
postmodern
romance

a maze of possibilities

■ Your turn - choose a
genre and adopt a style
you haven't tried before.
Begin writing a novel,
setting up some separate
chapters. Write a section
with a historical or
romantic influence. Have
fun with a 'Mills and
Boon' treatment! Try the
same piece using a Gothic
or science fantasy method.

stretch
the
envelope

the art of the interview
you are a journalist

Start by interviewing a member of the family. You'll need a series of questions but also the flexibility to adapt to the way the conversation might go.

Ask your interviewee to choose a suitable place (a kitchen table, a comfortable chair), share a cup of coffee, ask permission to use a video or audio recorder. Once the questions begin, you'll be surprised how lively the talking can become! An older family member often appreciates the opportunity to share memories.

writing up the interview

Listen to your recording and write down those parts of the conversation you want to keep. Here, editing is important - pauses and repetitions need to be eliminated and the more interesting details highlighted.

You can choose different methods for writing up your piece. How about the direct option, a straightforward record of discussion? Or set the scene by describing the interview complete with emotions and actions.

stretch the envelope

A. The interview as record:

S.B.: So where did you go to school?
D.M.: I went to Bendigo Primary School in the
sixties but later we moved to the city
and I went to a much larger school.
S.B.: Take us back. Are your memories of
country school life happy ones?

B. The interview as scenario:

The room Drusilla ushered me into was quite
small and cluttered; magazines were scattered
on the piano and the floorboards were
covered with a fine film of dust. Drusilla was
taller than I had imagined, but she had a
direct style that I recognised in my mother. I
wasn't sure what angle to begin with or how
she felt about being interviewed. I tentatively
asked her about her childhood in Cyprus and
she began talking.

Drusilla's story in her own words.

End on your reflections of the experience.

Once you've worked out a good technique,
move on to interviews with unfamiliar people
who have done something interesting – an
award-winner, a local politician, an actor.

make
your opinion
count

Your neighbourhood is a fertile ground for local debate. Find a copy of your local paper and draw up a list of social issues raised by journalists in their articles and by the public in the letters to the editor section.

environmental issues
planning a skateboard park
building facilities - old age home, kindergarten
lectures at the local library

■ Research your area of interest by gathering material from the library, newspapers and websites. Interview an involved person. After refining your ideas, write a letter or an opinion article and send it to the editor of the paper.

your sources

Ideas come from all directions. Sources include:
newspapers
magazines
libraries
internet

be a film critic

Check the Film Guide in your newspaper and read as many film reviews as you can.
Write notes on a film you have seen, checking first that you have recorded the credits accurately - names of actors, film title, director, cinematographer, music direction.

Steps to writing a film review – establish your ideas on:

location
genre
historical/ social context
characterisations
viewpoint/s
dramatic conflict
tone - serious, humorous, ironic
special effects - lighting/ camera style/editing
key scenes and overall evaluation - how successful is the film? Director's intention?
Compare with films on a similar subject or by the same director.

Your opinion is as valid as anyone else's!

publish
your work

Publishing your work brings your efforts to a satisfying and well-deserved end - enjoy a feeling of accomplishment by sharing with your audience. The cream on your coffee.

Private audience

chat rooms on the net
pen pals, sending letters and emails

Public audience

magazines
local paper/ enter competitions
publishing

how to present your writing

made by hand

**handmade paper
drawings
illustrations
photographs**

■ **Buy an attractive journal and stick
your pieces in. Begin with a contents
page. Put photos or drawings between
your stories. Decorate the margins.
Include photos of yourself.**

■ **A fun idea: Glue coloured envelopes of
different shapes to the pages. Fold a
separate story or poem in each envelope.
These are your personal satchels.
Someone else can unwrap them.**

digital presentation

**word process
import graphics
digital imaging
web design**

■ **Print copies of your
collected writings. Use special paper and
import digital images if you like. Spiral
bind each set of stories or investigate
other types of binding.**

■ **Publish on the Internet/ download your
stories on a disk/ burn a CD.**

■ **Give your book to your parents,
grandparents, friends.**
■ **Give your book as a gift with a
personal note.**

a star be a star be a star be a star be a star! be a star be a star be a star be a star be a star be a star be a star be a star be a star be star be a star be a star be a star be ar be a star be a star be a star be a st a star be a star be a star be a star be a star be a star be a star be a star be a star be

Be a star!

references

Astley, Thea, *The multiple effects of rainshadow*, Viking, Australia, 1996

Conrad, Joseph, *Heart of Darkness*, Penguin, Australia, 1995

Dessaix, Robert, *Night Letters*, Picador, Sydney, 1996

Gildiner, Catherine, *Too close to the falls*, Flamingo, London, 1999

Lorenzo, Olga, *The Rooms in My Mother's House*, Penguin, Australia, 1996

MacLeod, Alistair, *No Great Mischief*, Vintage, Great Britain, 2000

Malouf, David, *Dream Stuff*, Vintage, London, 2000

Malouf, David, *Fly Away Peter*, Penguin, Australia, 1983

Proulx, Annie E., *Heart Songs*, Allen & Unwin, NSW, 1994

Shreve, Anita, *Sea Glass*, Little, Brown, Great Britain, 2002

Williams, Niall, *Four letters of love*, Picador, London, 1997

index

■ Activities

Inspiration is a
sudden flash from a clear sky
strong and growing awareness
vivid and original insight
state of understanding.